2 YEAR

Class

Non-fiction Texts

Julie Orrell

Published in 2004 by:
Nelson Thornes Ltd
Delta Place
27 Bath Road
CHELTENHAM
GL53 7TH
United Kingdom

04 05 06 07 08 / 10 9 8 7 6 5 4 3 2 1

A catalogue record for this book is available from the British Library

ISBN 0-7487-8654-6

Illustrations by Alex Machin, Sally Michel, Nick Schon
Page make-up by GreenGate Publishing Services

Printed in Great Britain by Ashford Colour Press

Acknowledgements
All texts written by and copyright Julie Orrell except:

'Modelling fun' taken from *Now Try This* by Nick Huckleberry Beak, Petra Boase,
Thomasina Smith, Jack Wadeson, published by Southwater, priced at £11.99;
'How to make a battery light show' taken from *The Ultimate Activity Book*
published by Southwater, priced at £12.95; 'Dictionary Extract' Reprinted by
permission of HarperCollins Publishers Ltd Copyright © Malcolm J.White, Malcolm
Seccombe 2000; 'The Wheel' from *The Eyewitness Guide: Invention* (Dorling
Kindersley 1991) Copyright © Dorling Kindersley 1991; 'Body Bits' Copyright ©
DK FindOut.

Photographs: Text 12 (fruit juice) Corel 465 (NT); Text 25 (Electromagnet)
Photodisc 31 (NT); Text 27 both photographs from Photodisc 40 (NT); Text 33 all
photographs from Stephen Frink/Digital Vision LU (NT); Text 38 (Chariot) Corel 473
(NT); Text 39 Plank Wheel (25013092) and Cross-Bar Wheel (20236298) copyright
© Dorling Kindersley.

Cover image: AA052313 © Getty/Photodisc Red/Bryan Mullennix (royalty free)
Soccer ball hitting inside of net

Every effort has been made to trace the copyright holders but if any have been
inadvertently overlooked, the publishers will be pleased to make the necessary
arrangement at the first opportunity.

Contents

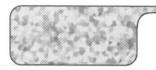

How to use this book

What this book contains	• Extracts from published works, plus tailor-made extracts, all arranged and chosen specifically to match the examples of medium-term planning provided by the National Literacy Strategy
	• Teaching ideas for each extract to get you started, covering some of the relevant text, sentence or word level objectives from the relevant unit
How you can use *Classworks Literacy Texts* with other resources	• The blocked unit structure means you can dip into the book to find resources perfect for what you're teaching this week – it doesn't matter what plan, scheme or other resource you're using
	• There are two *Classworks Literacy Texts* books for every year from Reception (or Primary 1) to Year 6 (or Primary 7): one contains Fiction and Poetry, the other contains Non-fiction. Both books together contain texts for every unit of the medium-term plans

What each page does

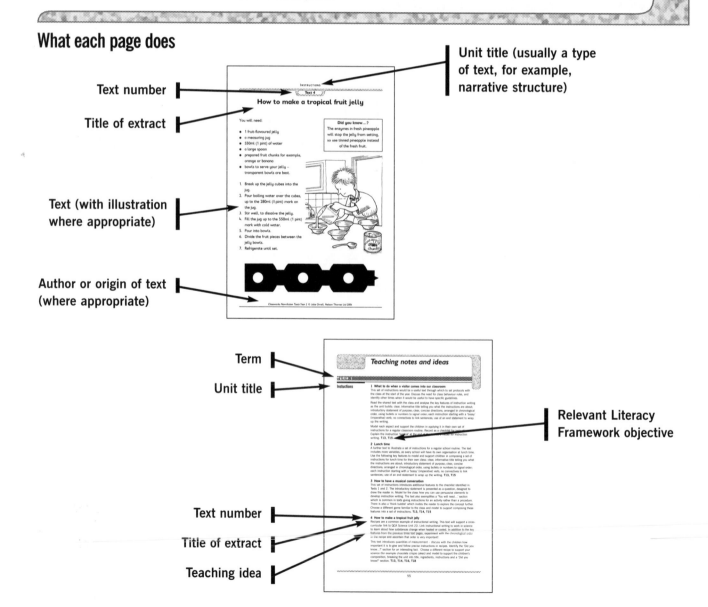

Text number

Title of extract

Text (with illustration where appropriate)

Author or origin of text (where appropriate)

Unit title (usually a type of text, for example, narrative structure)

Term

Unit title

Relevant Literacy Framework objective

Text number

Title of extract

Teaching idea

Text I

What to do when a visitor comes into our classroom

People often come into the classroom to learn about what we are doing at school. Help them enjoy their visit by following these simple instructions!

1 Carry on sensibly with what you are doing when a visitor comes into the classroom.
2 Don't interrupt your teacher if they are talking to the visitor, wait until they have finished speaking if you need help.
3 Try to sort out any problems yourself if you can.
4 Work quietly.
5 Listen carefully to questions that the visitor asks.
6 Answer the questions politely and explain what you are doing.

If you follow these instructions, visitors will be able to enjoy learning about our school.

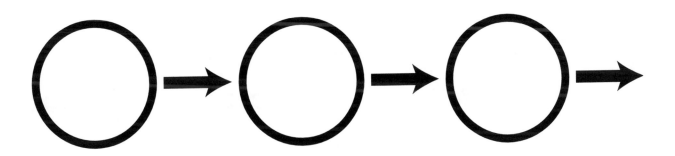

Text 2

Lunch time

A set of lunch instructions to help make happy lunch times!

1   Line up quietly by the door when you hear the bell.
2   Fetch your lunchbox and go to the hall, if you are having a packed lunch.
3   Put on your coat and go out to play if you are having a school lunch.
4   Line up sensibly when it is your turn for school lunch.
5   Take a tray and cutlery from the trolley.
6   Ask politely for the food that you choose.
7   Remember to say "Thank you".
8   Eat your lunch quietly and sensibly.
9   Put your tray and cutlery away when you have finished.

Remember – following the rules makes lunch time happy for everyone!

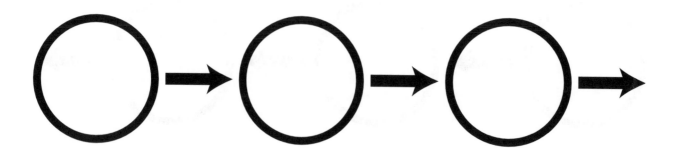

How to have a musical conversation

Is it possible to have a conversation without words? Try this game!

You will need:

- 2 pitched percussion instruments using only notes C, D, E, G, A
- 2 beaters

1 Sit in a big circle, with the instrument in the middle.
2 Choose two children at a time to sit facing one another, each holding a beater.
3 Use only your instrument to communicate with your partner.
4 Take it in turns to play, only one instrument can play at any time.
5 Listen carefully to your partner's musical message before you reply.
6 After one minute, swap for another pair to have a conversation.

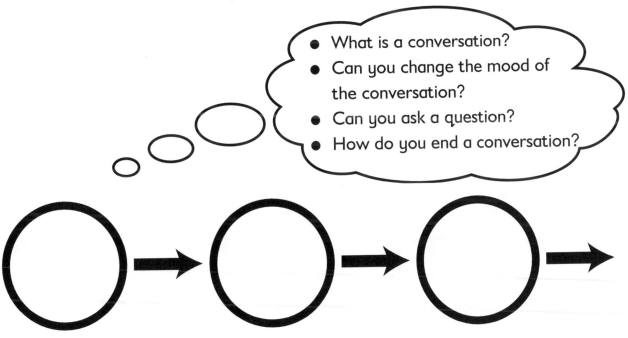

- What is a conversation?
- Can you change the mood of the conversation?
- Can you ask a question?
- How do you end a conversation?

Classworks Non-fiction Texts Year 2 © Julie Orrell, Nelson Thornes Ltd 2004

How to make a tropical fruit jelly

You will need:

- 1 fruit-flavoured jelly cubes
- a measuring jug
- 550ml (1 pint) of water
- a large spoon
- prepared fruit chunks, for example, orange or banana
- bowls to serve your jelly – transparent bowls are best.

1. Break up the jelly cubes into the jug.
2. Pour boiling water over the cubes, up to the 280ml (½ pint) mark on the jug.
3. Stir well, to dissolve the jelly.
4. Fill the jug up to the 550ml (1 pint) mark with cold water.
5. Pour into bowls.
6. Divide the fruit pieces between the jelly bowls.
7. Refrigerate until set.

Did you know...?
The enzymes in fresh pineapple will stop the jelly from setting, so use tinned pineapple instead of the fresh fruit.

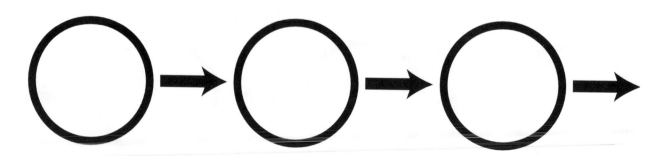

Modelling Fun
Grinning Cat

This grinning cat looks very pleased with itself. You can almost hear it purring! This model is very simple to make because the cat's legs are curled tightly under its body. Do not make the tail too thin or it will break.

YOU WILL NEED THESE MATERIALS AND TOOLS

Modelling tool   White drying modelling material

PVA Glue   Paintbrush   Acrylic paints

1   Roll a ball of white drying modelling material between your palms to make the head. Then roll a thick sausage 6 cm (2½ in) long and 2½ cm (1 in) wide for the cat's sleek body.

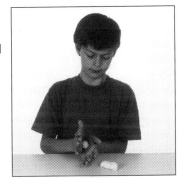

2   To fix the head on to the body, score the bottom of the head with the modelling tool and press the head firmly on to the body. Smooth the join with your fingers.

3   Cut and shape two pieces of modelling material to make the front paws. Press them into position. Make a tail and press it on to the body. Curl the tail around the body.

Petra Boase

Classworks Non-fiction Texts Year 2 © Julie Orrell, Nelson Thornes Ltd 2004

Text 6

Modelling Fun (continued)

4   Flatten a small piece of modelling material with the palm of your hand. Use the blade of the modelling tool to cut out two small triangles for the cat's ears.

5   Use the modelling tool to carve the features of the cat. You might want to practise this using a piece of leftover material. Allow the cat to dry for about 12 hours before starting to paint it.

6   Carefully paint the cat and use only the very boldest colours. Allow the paint to dry thoroughly before applying a varnish made of 8 parts PVA glue and 1 part water.

Paperweight Cat

Because Grinning Cat does little more all day than sit around looking pleased with itself, it would make a great paperweight. A paperweight stops sheets of paper from being blown around and lost. To make Paperweight Cat, all you have to do is make a larger and therefore heavier model. You will need to allow 24 hours for drying before painting.

Petra Boase

Classworks Non-fiction Texts Year 2 © Julie Orrell, Nelson Thornes Ltd 2004

Text 7

How to make a battery light show

Electricity is stored in the battery. It can only move, or flow, when it has a complete circle, or circuit, to go around. This circuit is made from wires, a switch and a bulb. When the switch is ON, the electricity goes from one end, or terminal, on the battery, along the wires, through the switch and light bulb, back to the battery's other terminal. As electricity goes through the bulb, it glows. When the switch is OFF, it makes a gap or break in the circuit. The electricity stops – and the light goes out.

YOU WILL NEED THESE MATERIALS AND TOOLS

9-volt battery
Wide coloured sticky tape
Yellow card
Scissors
PVA glue
Small torch bulb and holder
3 pieces of plastic coated wire with ends bared
Screwdriver
Small piece of card
Paper clip
Split pins
Coloured dot stickers

> **WARNING**
> NEVER TOUCH
> ELECTRICAL WIRES,
> SWITCHES, PLUGS
> OR SOCKETS
> WITHOUT HELP
> FROM A GROWN-UP.

1   Decorate the battery to make it look powerful by winding a piece of wide coloured sticky tape right around it.

2   Cut out some zig-zag "lightning flashes" from the yellow card and stick them onto the sides of the battery with glue.

Steve and Jane Parker

Text 8

How to make a battery light show (continued)

3 Screw the light bulb into the holder. Push the end of a piece of wire under one of the connecting screws. Screw it down. Repeat with another piece of wire under the other screw.

4 Take the end of one of these pieces of wire and twist it onto one of the battery terminals (the bits of metal on the top of the battery).

5 Twist the end of the third piece of wire onto the other battery terminal. Make sure that both these wires grip the terminals tightly.

6 Push two holes in the piece of card, the length of the paper clip apart. Push a split pin through one hole. Push the other split pin through the paper clip and then through the other hole. Open the ends of the pins under the card. This is the switch.

7 Twist one free wire end around one split pin and the other around the other split pin. When the paper clip touches both split pins, the switch is ON (green dot) and the light bulb shines. When the paper clip is moved away from the split pin, the switch is OFF (red dot).

Steve and Jane Parker

Using a dictionary

What is a dictionary?

A dictionary is an information text that contains lots of words and their definitions. Dictionaries can be very big, containing all the words that are used in our language. Dictionaries can also be collections of words used for a particular subject, or words used by readers of different ages.

How is a dictionary organised?

All dictionaries are organised in alphabetical order. This means that the order of letters in the alphabet is used to arrange the words.

a b c d e f g h i j k l m
n o p q r s t u v w x y z

If more than one word starts with the same letter, then we need to look at the second or maybe even further letters to get the order right. The alphabet is used to put the words in order.

game
gate
glue
goat
green

When do we need to use a dictionary?

There are several uses of a dictionary.

1   To find out the meaning of a word that we have not come across before.
2   To find out how to spell a word if we are not sure of the spelling.
3   Some dictionaries tell us how to pronounce a tricky word.
4   Some dictionaries tell us the part that the word plays in a sentence, for example, whether it acts as a verb, adjective or noun.

Classworks Non-fiction Texts Year 2 © Julie Orrell, Nelson Thornes Ltd 2004

Text 10

Using a dictionary (continued)

How do we use a dictionary?

Use your knowledge of alphabetical order to find your word.

Next to the word you will see all the information for that word.

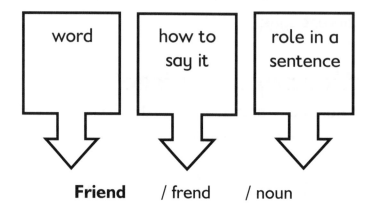

| word | how to say it | role in a sentence |

Friend   / frend   / noun

1   A person you know and like.

2   A person on the same side in a struggle, an ally.

3   A supporter.

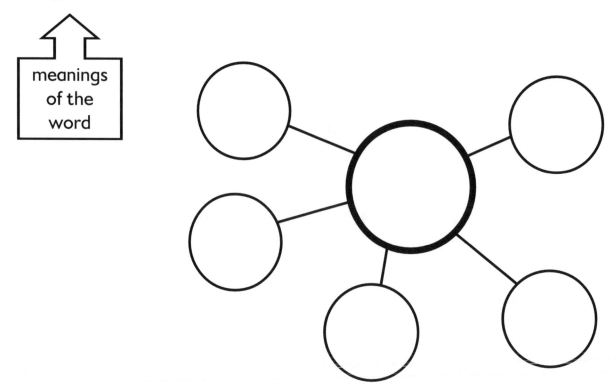

meanings of the word

Text 11

Dictionary extract

jacket jackets

NOUN

1   A jacket is a short coat.

EXAMPLE He wore a leather jacket.

2   A jacket is an outer covering for something.

EXAMPLE The book jacket was very colourful.

January

NOUN

January is the first month of the year.

EXAMPLE Snow fell throughout January.

Jew Jews

NOUN

A Jew is someone who believes in Judaism; also someone of Hebrew descent.

EXAMPLE Both Jews and Muslims live in Jerusalem.

join joins joining joined

VERB

1   When two things join they come together.

EXAMPLE This road eventually joins the motorway.

Similar words connect, link, unite

2   If you join a club or organisation, you become a member of it.

EXAMPLE He joined the Army five years ago.

Malcolm White and Malcolm Seccombe

Dictionary extract (continued)

Journey journeys

> *NOUN*
>
> A journey is the act of travelling from one place to another.
>
> EXAMPLE It was a long journey to the hotel.

Judaism

> Said: joo-day-i-zm
>
> *NOUN*
>
> Judasim is the religion of the Jewish people, which is based on a belief in one God.
>
> EXAMPLE The Hebrew Scriptures tell how Judaism began.

juice juices

> *NOUN*
>
> Juice is the liquid that can be obtained from fruit or other food.
>
> EXAMPLE He has orange juice with his breakfast.

Malcolm White and Malcolm Seccombe

Text 13

Glossary of terms for wildlife in our local environment

Antenna A feeler on the head that can detect touch, smell or taste.

Camouflage When an animal is patterned, coloured or shaped to blend in with its environment.

Carnivore An animal that eats the meat of other animals.

Compound eye An eye made up of separate units. Insects have compound eyes.

Evolution The way living things change over time. New species develop, other species die out and become extinct.

Extinction When all of a species has died out.

Eye The part of the body that detects light and sends signals to the brain.

Food chain The relationship between living things through food. Animal life depends on many food chains.

Gills Feathery slits that absorb the oxygen in water. Fish breathe through gills.

Habitat A particular natural environment suited to certain plants and animals. Woodlands, ponds and seashores are habitats.

Hibernation A deep sleep used by warm-blooded animals in cold weather.

Glossary of terms for wildlife in our local environment (continued)

Insectivore An animal that eats mainly insects.

Invertebrate An animal without a backbone.

Larva The growing stage that follows the egg stage in certain animals.

Metamorphosis When an animal changes its body shape as it grows, such as a butterfly.

Nutrients Substances taken in as food by living things to help them grow.

Omnivore An animal that eats both meat and plants.

Oxygen An invisible gas needed by all living things.

Predator An animal that hunts prey for food.

Prey An animal hunted by a predator.

Pupa The resting stage of creatures such as butterflies. It is sometimes called a chrysalis or a cocoon.

Territory An area that an animal lives in and defends against intruders.

Vertebrate An animal with a backbone. The main groups of vertebrates are fish, mammals, amphibians, reptiles and birds.

Warning colours Bright colours and patterns on an animal's body which act as a warning that they are harmful to eat.

Glossary of terms for science work on materials

Cardboard

Stiffened paper, made from wood pulp. Most boxes are made of cardboard as it is stronger than paper.

Clay

Earth that can be moulded into shape. Clay hardens when heated and is used to make crockery.

Fabric

A material made from cotton, wool or silk, or is man-made, such as nylon. Clothes are made of fabric.

Glass

A hard, brittle substance that is transparent and very fragile. Windows are made of glass.

Paper

A thin, flexible material made from wood pulp.

Plastic

A synthetic material that can be moulded into shape.

Rubber

An elastic substance, formed from the milky sap of the rubber plant.

Substance

A material.

Synthetic

A substance that is artificial, that has been produced by man.

Wood pulp

Ground up wet fibres of wood, from which paper is made.

Classworks Non-fiction Texts Year 2 © Julie Orrell, Nelson Thornes Ltd 2004

Glossary of terms for map-making

Altitude

Height above sea level.

Atlas

A collection of maps.

Compass

A device for measuring direction. Compass points on a map show which way is north.

Continent

A large area of land. The Earth is divided into continents.

Co-ordinates

Two reference numbers which cross to give an exact point on a grid.

Direction

Measured by a compass. Compass points are north, south, east and west.

Equator

An imaginary circle around the middle of the Earth.

Globe

A three-dimensional spherical map of the Earth.

Grid

A pattern of lines on a map to help give an exact location.

Key

This tells you what the symbols on a map mean.

Map

A two-dimensional picture of a place, drawn to scale.

Scale

The relationship in size between a distance on a map and the same distance on the ground.

The life cycle of a frog

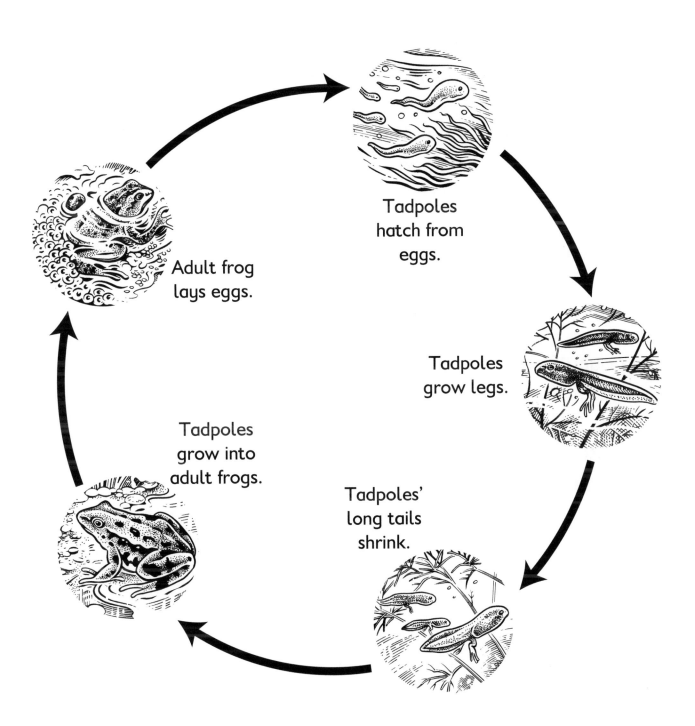

Tadpoles hatch from eggs.

Tadpoles grow legs.

Tadpoles' long tails shrink.

Tadpoles grow into adult frogs.

Adult frog lays eggs.

Classworks Non-fiction Texts Year 2 © Julie Orrell, Nelson Thornes Ltd 2004

Text 18

The life cycle of a frog
(continued)

Frogs are amphibians. They live both on the land and in the water. Frogs lay their eggs in the water.

The adult frog lays eggs inside jelly balls, called frogspawn.

When the eggs hatch, tiny tadpoles eat their way out of the jelly. This provides their first food.

As the young tadpoles begin to grow, they start to grow legs and turn into little frogs.

Next their long tails start to shrink.

The young frogs grow into adult frogs and can then mate and lay eggs of their own.

If we look at this as a flowchart it makes a circle, or life cycle.

What is a food chain?

Living things need energy as food. A food chain passes energy along from one living thing to another as food.

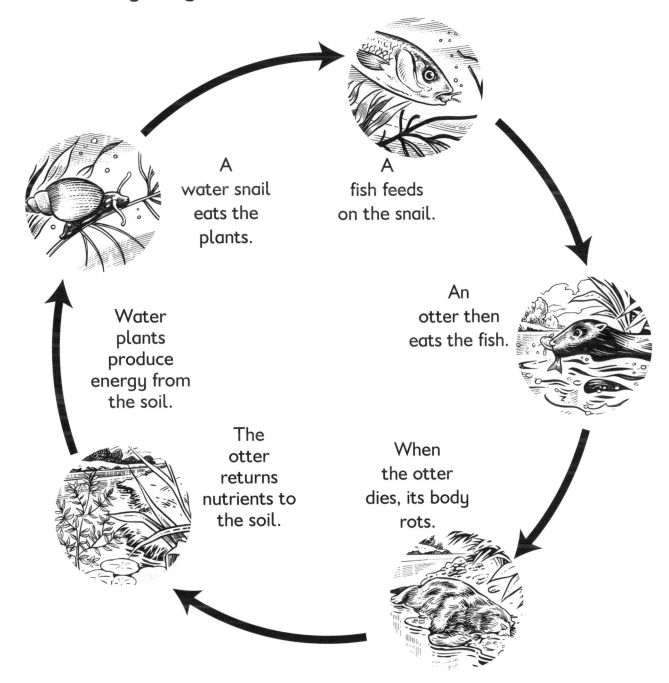

A water snail eats the plants.

A fish feeds on the snail.

An otter then eats the fish.

Water plants produce energy from the soil.

The otter returns nutrients to the soil.

When the otter dies, its body rots.

All life is dependent upon food chains to survive. Animals and plants can belong to many different food chains.

Making a marble run

Marble run challenge

How does the height of a marble run affect the speed of the marble?

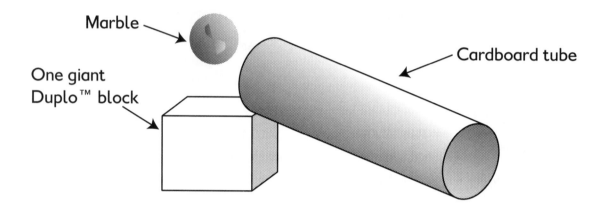

When we use one block, the marble only runs five metres.
The slope isn't very steep.

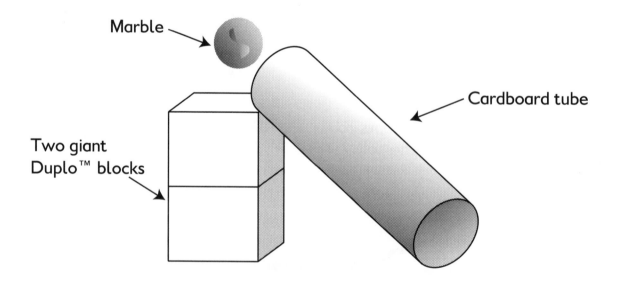

The marble run with two blocks makes the marble travel
nine metres. It goes further because the slope of the tube is
steeper and so the marble runs faster.

How water changes when heated or cooled

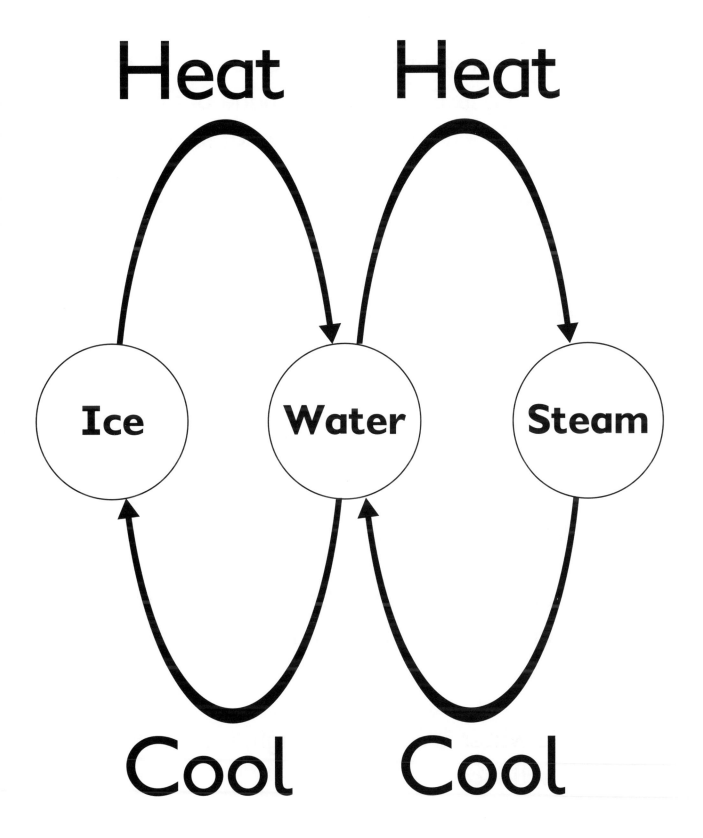

How water changes when heated or cooled
(continued)

Water has three states: solid, liquid and gas. We can change liquid water into a solid by cooling it, and into a gas by heating it. Everything is made of tiny particles, which can change when heated or cooled.

Ice is a solid. Solids like ice can be changed into liquids by heating them. When ice is heated, its particles move further apart until they can slide over each other and the ice turns into a liquid.

Liquids flow and fit the shape of any container. Liquids can be changed by heating them and making their particles move further apart. All liquids turn into gases when you heat them. When you heat liquid water, it turns into steam.

Steam, or water vapour, is a gas. It is invisible. All gases turn back into liquids again when they are cooled.

When liquid water is cooled enough, it turns from a liquid into solid ice.

How to use these information pages

These texts give information on different subjects that you will be interested in finding out about.

You will find information both in the photographs and illustrations, and in the words. This page explains how an information text works.

The **main text** on each page provides you with a short introduction to the subject (in **bold**) followed by further, more detailed information.

Illustrations give you information to explain the text. The illustrations are clear and easy to understand.

Captions label parts of a picture.

The Glossary box gives you the meaning of words in the text that you may not have come across before.

A **'Did you know...?'** box gives you an interesting and unusual fact about the subject.

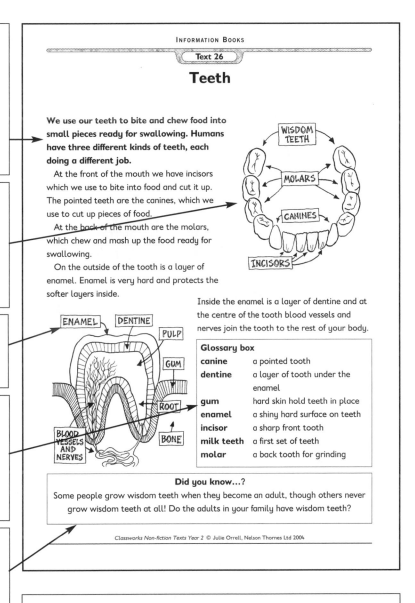

Teeth

We use our teeth to bite and chew food into small pieces ready for swallowing. Humans have three different kinds of teeth, each doing a different job.

At the front of the mouth we have incisors which we use to bite into food and cut it up. The pointed teeth are the canines, which we use to cut up pieces of food.

At the back of the mouth are the molars, which chew and mash up the food ready for swallowing.

On the outside of the tooth is a layer of enamel. Enamel is very hard and protects the softer layers inside.

Inside the enamel is a layer of dentine and at the centre of the tooth blood vessels and nerves join the tooth to the rest of your body.

WISDOM TEETH

MOLARS

CANINES

INCISORS

ENAMEL DENTINE PULP

GUM

ROOT

BLOOD VESSELS AND NERVES BONE

Glossary box

canine	a pointed tooth
dentine	a layer of tooth under the enamel
gum	hard skin hold teeth in place
enamel	a shiny hard surface on teeth
incisor	a sharp front tooth
milk teeth	a first set of teeth
molar	a back tooth for grinding

Did you know...?

Some people grow wisdom teeth when they become an adult, though others never grow wisdom teeth at all! Do the adults in your family have wisdom teeth?

Classworks Non-fiction Texts Year 2 © Julie Orrell, Nelson Thornes Ltd 2004

Photographs on some pages give the reader a picture of what things actually look like and can provide more information than words alone.

Magnets

Magnets attract metal objects towards them through a force we call magnetism. We can use this force in all sorts of ways, from lifting heavy objects to keeping the fridge door shut.

A magnet has a north pole at one end, and a south pole at the other. These poles work in opposite ways, the north pole of one magnet will pull the south pole of another towards it.

The Earth itself works as a giant magnet, with poles at the top and bottom of the planet.

North pole

South pole

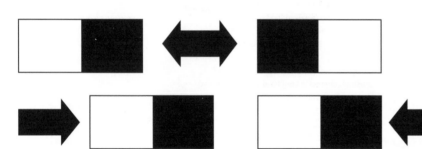

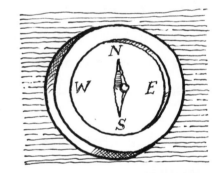

A compass is used to show directions. The needle of the compass works as a little magnet, which will always swivel to face the North Pole. To use a compass, turn it so that the needle is in line with the north symbol "N" and this will show you where the other directions are.

Glossary box

compass	a magnetic needle to show north
electromagnet	a magnet caused by electricity
magnetism	the pulling force of magnets.
poles	the opposite ends of a magnet

Did you know...?

In the past, sailors and explorers used compasses to plot their journeys as there were few accurate maps and charts. People still use them today to find directions.

Magnets (continued)

Many metal objects are magnetic, but not all. You can test a metal object to see if it is magnetic by placing it near a magnet. If the object is magnetic, it will be drawn towards the magnet. Objects made from other materials such as plastic, glass or wood are not magnetic.

Magnetic objects

The power of magnets can cause damage to other electrical items, so make sure that you keep them away from computers, videos and tapes.

Giant magnets are used to move heavy objects. Cranes in shipyards lift heavy containers onto boats using huge magnets. In scrapyards, big magnets on cranes lift the large lumps of metal around.

When electricity is passed through a wire it makes the wire magnetic. This is used to make electromagnets, which become magnetic only when the electricity is switched on. These electromagnets are very powerful and can lift big weights.

If you use a strong magnet, it will pull an object even through other materials. Try covering a table with paper and drawing a road track. Using a strong magnet, see how many ways you can control the car using the magnet.

Teeth

We use our teeth to bite and chew food into small pieces ready for swallowing. Humans have three different kinds of teeth, each doing a different job.

At the front of the mouth we have incisors which we use to bite into food and cut it up. The pointed teeth are the canines, which we use to cut up pieces of food.

At the back of the mouth are the molars, which chew and mash up the food ready for swallowing.

On the outside of the tooth is a layer of enamel. Enamel is very hard and protects the softer layers inside.

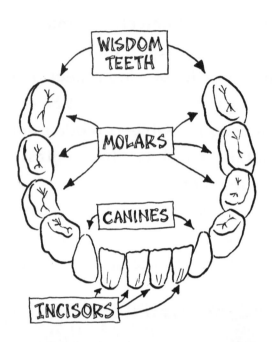

Inside the enamel is a layer of dentine and at the centre of the tooth blood vessels and nerves join the tooth to the rest of your body.

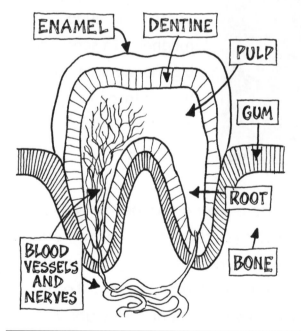

Glossary box	
canine	a pointed tooth
dentine	a layer of tooth under the enamel
gum	hard skin hold teeth in place
enamel	a shiny hard surface on teeth
incisor	a sharp front tooth
milk teeth	a first set of teeth
molar	a back tooth for grinding

Did you know...?

Some people grow wisdom teeth when they become an adult, though others never grow wisdom teeth at all! Do the adults in your family have wisdom teeth?

Classworks Non-fiction Texts Year 2 © Julie Orrell, Nelson Thornes Ltd 2004

Teeth (continued)

It is very important to clean your teeth every day. Cleaning your teeth removes the sugar and bacteria that collect on your teeth when you eat.

When you visit the dentist, your teeth will be checked to make sure that they are growing correctly and that there are no signs of decay. It is important that you visit the dentist regularly so that your teeth stay healthy.

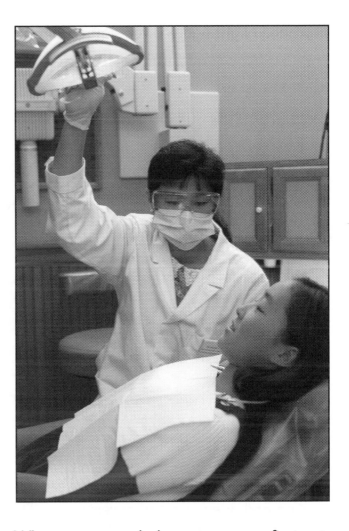

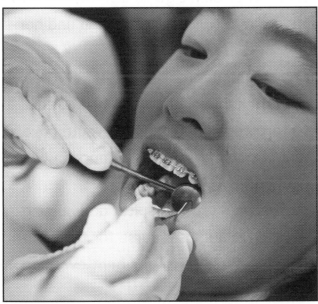

When you are a baby you grow a first set of teeth, called milk teeth. Children have 20 milk teeth.

At the age of 6 or 7, milk teeth start to fall out and 32 permanent teeth grow in their place.

Sometimes children need to wear a brace, to make crooked teeth grow straight.

When teeth are lost through accidents or in old age, the dentist can make a false tooth that looks just like the original.

Recount of the life of Florence Nightingale – the lady of the lamp

Florence Nightingale is remembered for a long lifetime of service to nursing.

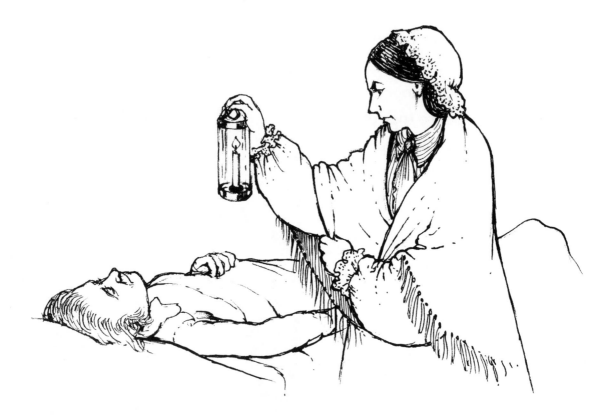

Florence Nightingale was born in Italy in 1820, in the city of Florence after which she was named. Her wealthy parents took Florence and her sister back to England while she was still small. When she was a young girl, Florence didn't go to school, but was taught at home by her father. Florence grew up into a clever young woman and her family expected her soon to marry.

Then in 1837, while she was in the garden at her home, Florence felt that she heard God calling to her and telling her to do his work. After this, she started visiting the sick people in the villages nearby. She became interested in nursing and would have liked to become a nurse. However, her family did not approve of this as nursing was not considered a suitable job for an educated woman.

In 1849 while travelling through Germany, Florence visited a hospital and nursing school. She decided to return the following year and trained as a nurse for three months. Next, Florence took a job as Superintendent of a hospital for gentlewomen in London.

Classworks Non-fiction Texts Year 2 © Julie Orrell, Nelson Thornes Ltd 2004

Recount of the life of Florence Nightingale (continued)

Three years later in 1854, Britain, France and Turkey declared war on Russia. This war was known as the Crimean War and many soldiers were injured and killed. Standards of medical care in army hospitals were poor and it was hard to keep wards hygienic and free from germs.

Meanwhile, Florence had been asked to go out to the military hospital in Scutari in Turkey, along with 38 female nurses. The idea of women being professional nurses was new to the doctors at the hospital but they soon realised how good they were at treating the sick. Although at first doctors were reluctant to accept their help, Florence and her team soon became very important to the wounded soldiers on the wards.

Florence Nightingale did much to improve the lives of those in the hospital. She set up reading rooms, and arranged for the soldiers' pay to be sent home to their loved ones. Florence and her nurses earned the respect of hundreds of wounded soldiers, who nicknamed her "the lady of the lamp".

After the end of the war in 1856 Florence returned home and worked to improve health conditions in all hospitals. In 1860, the Nightingale Training School for Nurses was set up, with Florence keeping a watchful eye on the trainee nurses. Her best known book, *Notes on Nursing,* was published in 1860.

For the next fifty years, Florence worked tirelessly to improve standards of health, both in hospitals and in the community. In 1883, Queen Victoria awarded Florence the Royal Red Cross and in 1907 she was the first woman ever to receive the Order of Merit. Florence died in 1910, aged ninety. She will be remembered for all she did to change health care and nursing.

Classworks Non-fiction Texts Year 2 © Julie Orrell, Nelson Thornes Ltd 2004

Text 30

Class 2 visit to the mosque

Last Friday Class 2 went to the mosque to visit a place of worship. We travelled to the mosque by coach, it took us half an hour to get there. The mosque was in the city centre.

First we took off our shoes and left them in a special entrance hall. There was a room for washing, because it is important to be clean before prayer.

Next we went into the Prayer Hall. It was very large and beautifully decorated. The walls were a golden colour and there were no pictures of Allah, as Muslims do not believe that God can be represented in human form. The ceiling was a domed shape, covered with patterns and arabic writing. On the floor were deep red prayer mats. There were no chairs as Muslims pray kneeling down. When praying, Muslims always face the same way towards Makkah. After that we saw the Qu'ran, which is the holy book.

Before we left to go back to school, we looked at the outside of the building. There was a big dome and a minaret tower.

When we returned to school we drew pictures to show what we had enjoyed about our visit. My favourite thing was the colourful patterns on the tiles. We learnt a lot about a Muslim place of worship on our visit to the mosque.

Text 31

Recount of the life of Louis Braille

Louis Braille is remembered for inventing the Braille alphabet, which gives blind people a system of reading and writing.

Louis Braille was born in France in 1809. He had an older brother and two older sisters and he lived in a farmhouse. His father was a leather craftsman who made saddles and harnesses for horses.

When he was a young child, Louis liked to help his parents at work on the farm. In 1812, when Louis was only three, there was a terrible accident. Louis was alone in his father's workshop. He had seen his father cut leather many times and wanted to try for himself. He took a sharp tool from the workbench and tried to make a hole in a piece of leather.

The next thing he knew was that the tool had slipped into his eye. Meanwhile, his parents who were working on the farm heard the screams and ran to the workshop. There was nothing that they or the doctors could do to save his eye. Soon, the infection spread to the other eye and Louis began to lose his sight. By the time he was five, Louis was completely blind.

When Louis was seven, he started going to the village school. Although he couldn't see, Louis could remember everything he heard. He did well at school, though it was difficult for him not to be able to read or write.

In 1819 Louis won a place at a special school for blind children in Paris. At the school, Louis found that there were books written in big, raised letters so that blind children could read them by feeling each letter. It took a long time to read each word!

Two years later, an army officer called Captain Barbier visited the school. He told the children about "night writing" – a system of writing which used holes punched into paper so that soldiers could communicate with each other at night. Louis wondered if this idea could help speed up the process of reading and writing for the blind.

Recount of the life of Louis Braille
(continued)

Louis worked on inventing his system. His dominoes gave him an idea. He wondered if letters could be represented by dots, a bit like the spots on a domino. After two years, he felt that he had invented a system of dots which would make reading much quicker. Now he was able to communicate with his school friends on paper.

Later, in 1828, Louis became a teacher at the school. His system of reading and writing was taught to pupils there, but outside the school few people were interested in his invention.

Louis Braille died in 1852, at the age of forty three. Two years later, his invention was at last recognised and used throughout France. It became known as Braille, after its inventor. Braille is now used across the world. Books, signs and computers use Braille to share information for the blind.

The Braille Alphabet

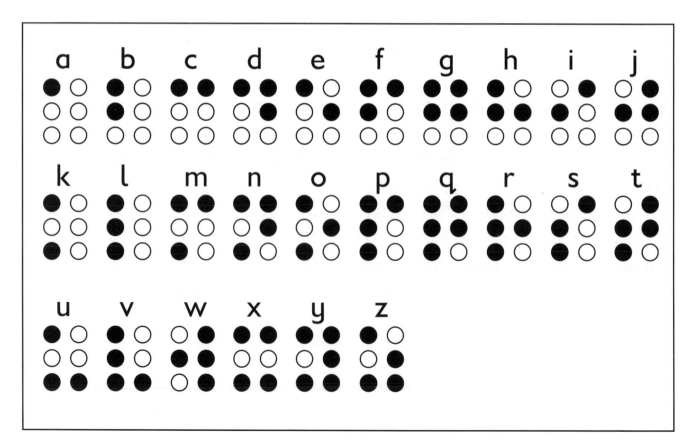

Visit Blue Water Aquarium

.... Blue Water Aquarium ....

Visit Blue Water Aquarium and take a look at the secret world of fish.

Come and explore the secret world under the water at the county's biggest aquarium. Wander through an incredible world teeming with sea life, from rockpool to deep ocean, as you follow the aquarium tour…

… rockpool wonders

Have you ever wondered what lives in a rockpool? Our seashore guide will introduce you to a world of shy, scuttling creatures and masters of disguise.

… city of sharks

Walk through the shark tunnel and share the wonder of the world's most famous fish.

… carnival of coral

The coral reefs of the world's warmer seas are home to a carnival of coloured fish,

from clowns to angels! Watch as they dance their way through the stacks of coral.

… seahorse magic

Did you know that in the world of seahorses it is the male who gives birth to the young? Find out more at our seahorse showcase.

… flight of the rays

Watch from under the tank as the majestic rays glide through the water like birds. Meet these fascinating fish close up in our long, low tanks.

By visiting Blue Water Aquarium, you are helping to look after this magical world. The staff at the Aquarium are committed to sea life conservation and will donate £1 from every entry fee to a marine conservation charity.

Visit Blue Water Aquarium
(continued)

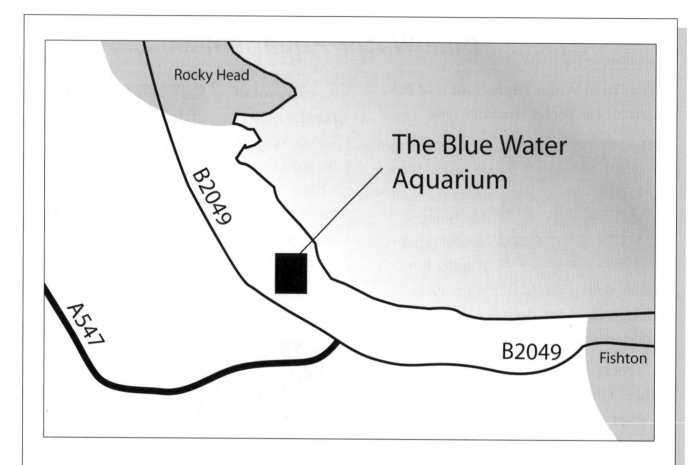

Where to find us

The Blue Water Aquarium is on the B2049 coast road between Rocky Head and Fishton. Parking is available at the rear of the Aquarium.

Opening hours

We are open EVERY DAY except Christmas Day and Boxing Day, from 10.00am to 5.00pm.

A tour of the Aquarium takes about two hours but you can stay as long as you wish.

Admission charges

Children 0–4 years free

Children 5–16 years   **£4.00**

Adults   **£5.00**

Why not have a meal at the Rockpool Café? Tea, coffee and soft drinks always available.

Extract from the diary of Samuel Pepys
September 2nd 1666

"So down [I went], with my heart full of trouble, to the Lieutenant of the Tower, who tells me that it began this morning in the King's baker's house in Pudding Lane, and that it hath burned St. Magnus's Church and most part of Fish Street already. So I rode down to the waterside, . . . and there saw a lamentable fire. . . Everybody endeavouring to remove their goods, and flinging into the river or bringing them into lighters that lay off; poor people staying in their houses as long as till the very fire touched them, and then running into boats, or clambering from one pair of stairs by the waterside to another."

Samuel Pepys

Finding out about the Great Fire of London

When did the fire take place?

It was early in the morning on the 2nd of September 1666 when the Great Fire started. It was a Sunday and because it was very early, people were asleep in their beds. The fire raged for four days until Thursday, when the last flames were put out.

Where did the fire start?

Fire broke out in a narrow street called Pudding Lane. The lane backed onto Fish Street Hill, which led to London Bridge itself. The fire started in the bakery of Thomas Farryner, the king's own baker.

Finding out about the Great Fire of London
(continued)

Why was the fire so devastating?

There are many reasons contributing to the spread of the fire.

1   Many buildings were made of timber and wattle-and-daub, which caught fire easily and helped to spread the flames. Roofs were often made of thatch, which set the sparks ablaze.

2   Streets were narrow and crowded, so it was easy for the flames to jump from house to house.

3   In 1666, London had no fire brigade. It was left to local people to deal with the fire, which they did by dousing the flames with water from hide buckets. The fire was rampaging so fiercely that they could not dampen the flames.

4   The Lord Mayor ordered citizens to pull down their houses to stop the path of the fire, but many refused.

5   A stiff east wind fanned the flames and spread the fire rapidly from street to street.

As a result of these factors, a small fire in a baker's shop grew into the Great Fire of London.

What happened as a result of the fire?

The fire destroyed more than 13,000 houses and many of London's important buildings. Eighty-seven churches burned down and after the fire many people were left homeless. Only five people are known to have died in the fire, one of whom was the maid at the bakery in Pudding Lane.

How do we know about the fire?

We have information about the fire from the diaries of Londoners who were alive at the time. The most famous of these was Samuel Pepys who saw the fire first-hand and wrote about it in his diaries. These diaries give us information about the past.

Text 38

The wheel

The wheel is probably the most important mechanical invention of all time. Wheels are found in most machines, in clocks, windmills, and steam engines, as well as in vehicles.

HISTORY OF THE WHEEL

STONE-AGE BUILDERS

Before the wheel, rollers made from tree trunks were probably used to push objects such as huge building stones into place. The tree trunks had the same effect as wheels, but a lot of effort was needed to put the rollers in place and keep the load balanced.

ROLLERS

Around 100 B.C. Danish wagon-makers may have tried putting wooden rollers around the axle in an attempt to make the wheel turn more smoothly.

WHEELS AT WAR

The wheel made possible the chariot, which originated in Mesopotamia around 2000 B.C.

THE FIRST WHEEL

The wheel first appeared in Mesopotamia, part of modern Iraq, over 5,000 years ago. It was used by potters to help work their clay, and at around the same time wheels were fitted to carts transforming transport and making it possible to move heavy materials and bulky objects with relative ease. These early wheels were solid, cut from sections of wooden planks which were fastened together. Spoked wheels appeared later, from around 2000 B.C. They were lighter, and were used for chariots.

The wheel (continued)

ROLLING STONE

In some places, where wood was scarce, stone was used for wheels instead. It was heavy, but long-lasting. The stone wheel originated in China and Turkey.

SCARCE BUT SOLID

Early wheels were sometimes solid discs of wood cut from tree trunks. These were not common as the wheel originated in places where trees were scarce. Solid wooden chariot wheels have been found in Denmark.

PLANK WHEEL

Three-part (or "tripartite") wheels were made of planks fastened together by wooden or metal cross-pieces. One of the earliest forms of wheel, they are still used in some countries. They are suitable for bad roads.

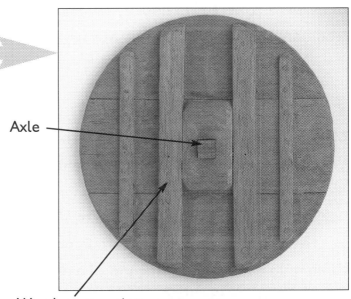

Axle

Wooden cross-piece

CROSS-BAR WHEEL

If large sections of a wheel were cut away, the wheel could be strengthened with struts or cross-bars. From here it was a small step to the spoked wheel we know today.

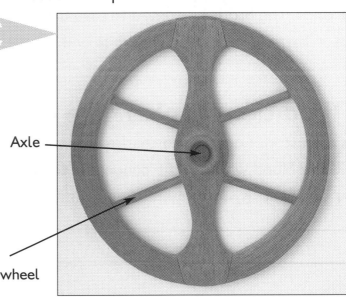

Axle

Spokes to strengthen wheel

Dorling Kindersley

Traditional tales

Many of our favourite stories are traditional tales. Children across the world have heard and enjoyed these stories for many generations.

What makes a story a traditional tale?

In the past, many people did not know how to read or write. Children did not have books to read or televisions to watch. Stories were told, rather than read and children enjoyed listening to the tales of their parents and grandparents. Long before these tales were collected in books they had been told by the fireside for generations. A traditional tale is a story that was first told, rather than written down.

Famous story tellers

Many of the world's traditional tales have been told and retold for hundreds of years. Each time they are told, they change a little in the telling – they are living stories. One of the first people to record tales in writing was Charles Perrault, a Frenchman who helped to build the famous palace at Versailles. His book called *Stories of Past Times,* written in 1697, contains eight traditional fairy tales including Little Red Riding Hood, Cinderella and Sleeping Beauty. The most famous storytellers of all are the Brothers Grimm. Early in the 1800s they began collecting traditional tales from their family and friends. The brothers wanted to save the stories they heard and write them down to stop them being lost. Snow White and Rumpelstiltskin are among their stories.

Traditional tales give a message

Often stories are told to children to warn them of dangers. The story of Little Red Riding Hood warns of the dangers of talking to strangers, and Cinderella tells us that a kind heart is worth more than riches.

Classworks Non-fiction Texts Year 2 © Julie Orrell, Nelson Thornes Ltd 2004

Traditional tales (continued)

Characters in traditional tales

Magical things happen in stories. In a fairy tale, anything can happen! Lands with castles appear above the clouds, animals talk, princes turn into frogs, fairy godmothers cast spells. Characters are either good or evil and usually the goodies win in a happy ending!

Fairy tale language

Because these tales are spoken tales, they have a special sort of language which lets you know that you are listening to an old, or traditional tale. Other written fairy tales use this language too, for they copy the style of the older traditional tales. Stories often start with "Once upon a time" or "Long, long ago" and they traditionally end with "and they all lived happily ever after".

Traditional tales have brought centuries of enjoyment to children all over the world.

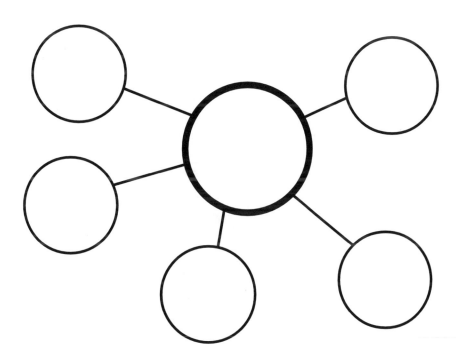

Body bits

Read about the skin you're in!

The skin is the largest human organ in the body – if you took it off, an adult's skin would cover two square metres and a child's skin would cover 1.5 square metres. It is also the heaviest part of the body and weighs between 2.5 and 4.5 kg depending on your size. Your "birthday suit" has a lot of important jobs, too. It keeps you the right temperature, protects you from germs and the Sun's rays and helps you "feel" things that you touch.

Bet you didn't know this..!
About 50,000 tiny flakes drop off your skin every minute.

In layers

Skin is less than 2 mm thick and has two clear layers. On top is the **epidermis**. Its upper part is made of flat, interlocking, dead cells, which are tough and waterproof. The cells are constantly worn away as skin flakes and are replaced by living cells in the lower epidermis.

Underneath the epidermis is the thicker **dermis**. The dermis contains sensors, nerves, blood vessels, sweat glands and hair roots.

Bet you didn't know this..!
Even after 4,000 years, you can still see the skin on Egyptian mummies.

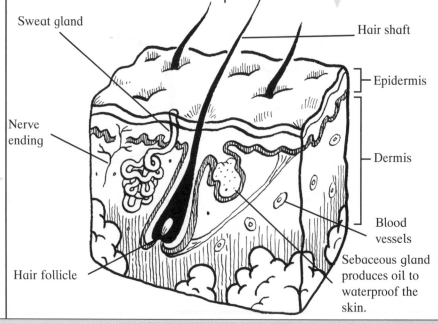

Sweat gland — Hair shaft — Epidermis — Nerve ending — Dermis — Hair follicle — Blood vessels — Sebaceous gland produces oil to waterproof the skin.

Tasha Browning

Classworks Non-fiction Texts Year 2 © Julie Orrell, Nelson Thornes Ltd 2004

Body bits (continued)

Cool it

Sweating helps to stop the body overheating when it gets hot. Normally the temperature in the body is a steady 37°C, but when you exercise, your hardworking muscles release heat. When the temperature in the body rises, the three million or so sweat glands in the skin release sweat. The sweat evaporates and

draws heat from the body to cool it down.

Melanin, a dark brown pigment made by cells in the skin, gives the skin its colour and protects it from the Sun's ultraviolet rays. Everyone needs to take care in the Sun, but very pale people need to take extra care because they have less melanin.

Make your mark

The lines and patterns on the ends of your fingers make up your fingerprints. Everybody's fingerprints are unique, with a different pattern of spirals, loops and arches. Sticky sweat is released onto the fingers which, along with the ridges, helps you to grip things.

Whenever people touch things, especially hard surfaces like metal or glass, they leave behind a copy of their fingerprints. Many criminals have been caught because they left their fingerprints behind at a crime scene.

Roll your finger on an inkpad and put your fingerprint here. Ask a friend to do the same and compare the patterns.

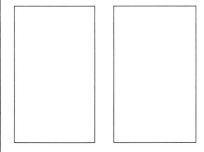

Ink can be messy, so make sure you ask an adult before you do this and wash your hands afterwards.

Tasha Browning

Butterflies and moths

Butterflies and moths make up the second largest insect group. They are called "Lepidoptera", which means "scaly winged" because of the tiny scales on four papery wings. There are around 175,000 types of butterflies and moths, living wherever there are trees and flowers.

Life cycle

Butterflies and moths go through a complete body change as they grow. This is called metamorphosis. Caterpillars emerge from eggs laid on a leaf. The caterpillar eats and grows. When it is too big for its skin it moults the skin and then eats and grows again. After the caterpillar has shed its last skin, it forms a hard case around itself and becomes a chrysalis, or pupa. Inside the hard case, the caterpillar's body changes into a butterfly. The butterfly emerges from the case, stretches its crumpled wings and flies away. In turn, this butterfly will lay its own eggs, making a life cycle.

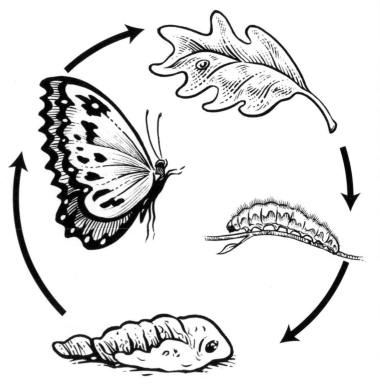

Butterfly or moth?

There are several differences between butterflies and moths. Moths are usually dull brown and grey colours, whereas butterflies are brightly coloured. Moths fly mainly at night, whereas butterflies are active in the day. Moths have feathery antennae, whereas butterflies have thin feelers with a bulb on the end.

Butterflies and moths (continued)

Warning colours

Caterpillars and butterflies often have bright stripes
to warn predators that they are harmful to eat. Some
butterflies have patterns that look like a large eye on
their wings to scare away predators. These are called
eye spots and are designed to look like the eye of an
owl or cat when the butterfly spreads its wings. Other
caterpillars and butterflies have colours that help them
merge into their habitats and camouflage themselves.

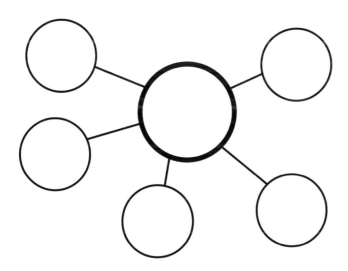

Food

Caterpillars spend much of their time eating leaves.
Often the eggs from which the caterpillars hatch have
been laid on exactly the right plant to be a food source
for them. Butterflies feed on the sweet, sugary nectar
deep inside flowers. Butterflies and moths have a very
long tube-shaped mouth which is kept coiled up under
their heads. To drink the nectar, the butterfly
straightens its mouth and uses it like a straw to sip up
the nectar.

Did You Know?

The insect with the
biggest wingspan is the
giant agrippa moth – its
wings measure 30cm
from tip to tip! See just
how big that is by
measuring it on a ruler!

Spiders

Spiders are arachnids which means that, unlike insects, they have eight legs and no wings. There are around 80,000 types of spider and they live all over the world in a wide range of habitats.

Spider silk

Spiders are unusual because of their ability to make a special silk thread with part of their body called a spinneret. Spiders use their silk for a wide range of purposes. The silk used to spin webs and trap prey is sticky and elastic. The silk used to wrap cocoons around their eggs to protect them is thick and smooth. Spiders also use silk for safety – to make silk parachutes for baby spiders so that they can blow in the wind to a new home and also to make safety ropes in case they should fall. Spider silk is one of the strongest materials known!

Webs

Spiders spin their silk into webs by firstly making a frame between two branches. The spider then spins radial threads, a bit like the spokes on a bicycle wheel. The final stage is to spin a spiral from the outside towards the centre, using sticky, elastic silk.

Spiders (continued)

Poisonous spiders

All spiders have poison in their bites but only a few have enough poison to harm humans. The most dangerous spiders have strong fangs and powerful poison. These spiders live in warm countries, like the Australian funnel web spider and the black widow spider.

Hidden danger

Some types of spider are very clever at snaring their prey. The trapdoor spider lives in burrows and uses its silk to make a trapdoor to cover the entrance. The spider lays silk threads as trip wires and as soon as it detects movement outside, it darts out of its burrow and bites the prey with its large fangs. The trapdoor spider then drags the prey back into its burrow and closes the trapdoor behind it.

Food

Most arachnids are predators and hunters. Their prey ranges from small insects to much larger creatures such as birds and mice. Some spiders, like the wolf spider, do not make webs but instead chase their prey across rocks and tree bark on their extra-long legs.

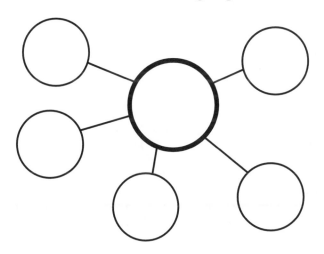

Did You Know?
The largest spider in the world is the goliath bird-eating spider from South America. It measures 28cm from the tip of one leg to the tip of the other. It preys on other spiders, lizards, birds and mice!

Text 48

How did the dinosaurs become extinct?

Dinosaurs became extinct about 65 million years ago. Nobody is exactly sure why this happened. Scientists have suggested these theories to explain their extinction.

One of the main theories is that a large meteorite hit the Earth 65 million years ago. The meteorite made a huge crater 180km wide which has been found on the seabed near Mexico. Some scientists believe that this caused a huge explosion, filling the air with dust and blocking out the Sun's light for months. Because the Earth became much colder, plants would have died. Without plants, plant-eating dinosaurs could not survive and the meat-eaters would have had no prey.

Some scientists believe that the Earth's climate changed because of the eruption of huge volcanoes. Volcanoes send up gases and dust into the atmosphere that first heat it up, then cool it down. This may have killed off the dinosaurs.

Classworks Non-fiction Texts Year 2 © Julie Orrell, Nelson Thornes Ltd 2004

How did the dinosaurs become extinct?
(continued)

The dinosaurs may have died out gradually. Dinosaurs would have moved across the land to find new feeding grounds as the climate grew cooler and the plants they were used to eating disappeared. The dinosaurs seem to have migrated south and it may be that they were not able to adapt to these changes.

One of the more unlikely theories is that the number of small mammals grew. These small animals liked to eat dinosaur eggs and this affected the number of dinosaur babies that hatched.

Millions of years ago, dinosaurs ruled the Earth. We know how they lived from the fossils dug up by palaeontologists but exactly how they died is still a mystery.

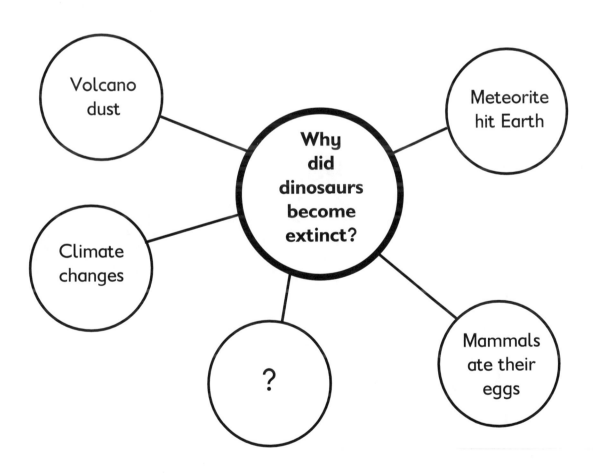

Text 50

A checklist for good speaking and listening

Good speakers:
- look at their listeners
- speak clearly
- speak audibly
- choose their words carefully
- organise their ideas so they make sense to the listener
- respond to what others say
- take turns to listen

Good listeners:
- look at the speaker
- use their faces to show that they are listening, for example, nodding
- think about what is being said
- ask questions to find out more
- comment and respond
- take turns to speak

Teaching notes and ideas

Instuctions

1 What to do when a visitor comes into our classroom

This set of instructions would be a useful text through which to set protocols with the class at the start of the year. Discuss the need for class behaviour rules, and identify other times when it would be useful to have specific guidelines.

Read the shared text with the class and analyse the key features of instruction writing as the unit builds: clear, informative title telling you what the instructions are about; introductory statement of purpose; clear, concise directions; arranged in chronological order, using bullets or numbers to signal order; each instruction starting with a 'bossy' (imperative) verb; no connectives to link sentences; use of an end statement to wrap up the writing.

Model each aspect and support the children in applying it in their own set of instructions for a regular classroom routine. Record as a checklist for instructions. Explain the instruction 'symbol' at the end of the text as a model for instruction writing. **T13, T15**

2 Lunch time

A further text to illustrate a set of instructions for a regular school routine. The text includes more variables, as every school will have its own organisation at lunch time. Use the following key features to model and support children in composing a set of instructions for lunch time for their own class: clear, informative title telling you what the instructions are about; introductory statement of purpose; clear, concise directions; arranged in chronological order, using bullets or numbers to signal order; each instruction starting with a 'bossy' (imperative) verb; no connectives to link sentences; use of an end statement to wrap up the writing. **T13, T15**

3 How to have a musical conversation

This set of instructions introduces additional features to the checklist identified in Texts 1 and 2. The introductory statement is presented as a question, designed to draw the reader in. Model for the class how you can use persuasive elements to develop instruction writing. The text also exemplifies a 'You will need...' section which is common in texts giving instructions for an activity rather than a procedure. There is also a 'think bubble' which invites the reader to explore the concept further. Choose a different game familiar to the class and model to support composing these features into a set of instructions. **T13, T14, T15**

4 How to make a tropical fruit jelly

Recipes are a common example of instructional writing. This text will support a cross-curricular link to QCA Science Unit 2D. Link instructional writing to work in science to learn about how substances change when heated or cooled. In addition to the key features from the previous three text pages, experiment with the chronological order in the recipe and ascertain that order is very important!

This text introduces quantities of measurement – discuss with the children how important it is to give and follow precise instructions in recipes. Identify the 'Did you know...?' section for an interesting fact. Choose a different recipe to support your science (for example chocolate crispie cakes) and model to support the children's composition, breaking the unit into title, ingredients, instructions and a 'Did you know?' section. **T13, T14, T16, T18**

Instructions containing diagrams

5–6 Modelling fun

The second unit on instruction writing moves from simple instructions to more complicated texts requiring explanatory pictures. Refer back to checklists made in the first unit and recap on features of instruction writing. Read the text and discuss how a combination of words and pictures can make the instructions clearer to the reader. Follow the instructions and make a grinning cat at the start of the unit, discussing detail and order. Using the text to support, write a class or individual set of instructions for making your clay model, focusing on the title, introductory statement, a 'You will need...' section (possibly illustrated) and numbered illustrated instruction boxes in chronological order. Reinforce the use of clear, concise language and bossy verbs with each instruction. **T17, T18**

7–8 How to make a battery light show

This text links to QCA Science Unit 2. Discuss the layout of the text; one page gives information, then the second page gives instructions. Identify that this format is an expanded version of the simple instructional texts studied earlier in the term. Build the unit by choosing a science experiment and modelling to support composition of title, technical explanation, 'You will need...' section, safety warning, numbered chronological instructions using technical language and accompanying pictures. Ensure that the children remember to use key features of instructional writing. **T17, T18**

TERM 2

Categorising alphabetically

9–10 Using a dictionary

Use this information text to introduce a unit on alphabetical ordering of words and their definitions (see Texts 11–12 for the dictionary extract). Look at a variety of dictionaries and identify common features and start a class checklist (in the children's own words) including the following:

- words are organised in alphabetical order. The order starts with the first letter in the word, then the second and so on;
- words are in bold type;
- words may be followed by a guide to pronunciation and may indicate the role the word plays in a sentence;
- the plural and other common variations may be listed;
- words are followed by meaning(s). Meanings are numbered if there are more than one;
- some dictionaries include an example of the word within a sentence;
- in picture dictionaries, some words are illustrated.

Use the dictionary extract, or an extract from a class dictionary, as a model to exemplify key features. Build individual dictionary pages from key features, with each child composing a page for a different letter of the alphabet. Compile in alphabetical order as a class dictionary.

11–12 Dictionary extract

This text provides an example of a dictionary page. Use to annotate the key features identified in Text 10 and to support the outcome of a class dictionary. **T16, T17, T20**

13–14 Glossary of terms for wildlife in our local environment

Define what a glossary is: a section of the text that gives definitions for words the author thinks may be difficult for the reader. Explore with the class how a glossary is different from a contents page and an index. Read Texts 44–45 on Butterflies and moths, and model for the class how you use this glossary to work out the meaning of some of the technical terms, for example, 'antenna', 'predator', 'camouflage', and 'metamorphosis'.

Discuss with the children that, when we are reading information books, some of the words may be unusual or scientific terms so we need a glossary to tell us exactly what they mean.

Use the text pages as a model to support in composing a class glossary of new vocabulary in an area of cross-curricular study. These texts support QCA Science Unit 2B. **T16, T17, T18, T20**

15 Glossary of terms for science work on materials

This text offers a further example of a glossary and would support QCA Science Unit 2D. **T16, T17, T18, T20**

16 Glossary of terms for map-making

This text offers an example of a glossary to support work in geography. **T16, T17, T18, T20**

Explanations

17–18 The life cycle of a frog

Explain to the class that an explanation is used to describe how something works or to explain a process in the natural world. An explanation may be in words, pictures or a combination of the two. In this text, the explanation of the life cycle of a frog is given in pictures, then in words. Discuss with the class how there is a general statement and then a series of steps to explain how or why it happens. Identify with the children that explanations are written in the present tense and compare this with recount where the past tense is used. Both text types use chronological order (as shown by connectives such as 'next', 'then' and 'when' to signal time) but an explanation text describes how something happens (present tense) rather than has happened (past tense). Use the text page to support in writing an explanation for a similar life cycle, for example that of a butterfly, building the unit by identifying, modelling and applying these text features. Texts 17 and 18 support QCA Science Units 2B and 2A. **T19, T21**

19 What is a food chain?
This text is a further example of a circular explanation, and could be used as a model to apply to a different food chain reflecting what is being taught in science. **T19, T21**

20 Making a marble run
This explanation text is constructed not as a circle, but rather as a comparison of two operations. The key features remain the same but the presentation of the explanation varies. Use the text to model for the class how we can use diagrams to explain forces by linking to QCA Science Unit 2E. *Developing Early Writing* Unit 13 provides exemplification of how to develop a unit of work on explanation at Year 2. **T19, T21**

21–22 How water changes when heated or cooled
This text represents a further example of how an explanation can be presented visually. **T19, T21**

TERM 3

Information books

To support this unit, a range of non-fiction text types are included to enable children to have access to differing information texts. In all of the text pages (23–35) links are made to QCA schemes of work. Implicit in all of these text types is the message that information texts give us facts, they are non-fiction. Secure the terminology 'fiction' and 'non-fiction' and reinforce throughout. **T13**

23 How to use this book

This text gives the reader information retrieval instructions. Note with the class how the title, introductory sentence, explanatory paragraph and central illustration with captions are explained. This text supports the following text pages on Teeth and Magnets. Use this page in conjunction with one of the texts to help the children find their way around the text. **T18**

24–25 Magnets

Discuss headings and introductory statements with the class, identifying how in this text the introductory statement gives a brief, general statement about magnets. Explore how the text is then divided into sections, identifying the sub-sections. Look with the class at how illustrations and captions are used to make the subject clearer to the reader. The 'glossary box' is a useful way to include specific vocabulary. **S9**

Using the layout exemplified, model for the class how you are going to make your own double-page information sheet on magnets on a large sheet of sugar paper. Build the composition following the sequence of title, heading, introductory statement, subtitles, pictures with captions, and a glossary box. The class could work in pairs on a large sheet of paper to compile their own information text as the unit builds. **T20**

26–27 Teeth

This text follows the same organisation as Texts 24–25.
Use Teeth to explore the use of information texts to answer questions. Generate a class list of questions about teeth:

- What is a tooth made of?
- When do we lose our baby teeth?
- What happens if teeth go bad?
- Why are sweets bad for our teeth?
- How many teeth have we got?
- What happens if our teeth don't grow straight?
- What are wisdom teeth?
- Why do we have to brush our teeth every day?

Write the questions on Post-it™ notes and divide between groups. Discuss the use of the question mark and secure formation. Working in pairs or small groups, challenge the children to find specific information to answer their questions. Provide copies of the text and highlighter pens for the groups to colour relevant information. Extend the question and answer model as the unit builds, supporting children in composing their own questions before searching for the answer in the text.

When the children have had an opportunity to pose and answer questions from the text, demonstrate for them how ICT can be used to ask questions on the Internet through a question-based search engine for children such as *www.ajkids.com*

At the end of the unit the children will have compiled a collection of questions and answers which can be organised into a 'lift the flap to find the answer' format and displayed. **S6, S7, T16, T14**

Texts 28–32 provide examples of recount as an information text which have cross-curricular links to Year 2 QCA Units.

28–29 Recount of the life of Florence Nightingale – the lady of the lamp

Explore with the class how recount is used to record a chronological series of events that took place in the past. Discuss how recount is 'factual', or 'non-fiction'. Read the text with the class and draw up a class timeline for Florence Nightingale. Arrange the eight key points in her life on Post-it™ notes along the line and use this as a visual representation for chronological ordering.

Explore the use of connectives to signal time, for example, 'then', 'meanwhile', 'later', 'after', 'for the next fifty years...' Compile a bank of connectives to signal time.

Model for your class how to compose a daily short paragraph or sentence for each of the eight sections, using a sheet of A3 paper folded into eight numbered squares to represent the eight sections. As the unit builds, explore and apply the use of time connectives, past tense, dates, technical language and model these to support the children in writing their own recounts. **T13, S3, W9**

30 Class 2 visit to the mosque

Use a class visit to explore how to recount personal events. This text links to QCA RE Unit 2D on visiting places of worship and can be used as a model to support a school visit. The key features of past tense, chronological order, time connectives and fact, not fiction, identified in the previous text are also present here.

31–32 Recount of the life of Louis Braille

The text provides a further model of a recount of a famous life. Explore the chronological organisation through sequencing major events in Louis' life and identify the connectives used to signal time. Build into a unit with an outcome of a report in pairs or groups to the rest of the class, in the style of a *Blue Peter* news report.

33–34 Visit Blue Water Aquarium

Texts 33–34 provide a different non-fiction text-type, introducing persuasive writing. Explore with the class how, although this is an information text, its purpose is to try to persuade as well as to inform. Identify with the class how the visual presentation of the information is important – an actual brochure would need to be bright, bold and colourful to attract the reader.

Discuss with the class how adjectives can be used to make places sound really exciting.

Collect examples of tourist information brochures from your local area and read in guided reading groups at different levels. Do they make you want to visit?
Choose a local landmark and design a brochure to persuade people to visit. Model each feature for the class as the unit builds, to support their own versions. **T18**

35 Extract from the diary of Samuel Pepys

This text supports Texts 36–37 on the Great Fire of London. Use the page in conjunction with these, as an information source. This extract is particularly useful for exploring new vocabulary. These text pages link to QCA History Unit 5.

Reports

The following texts are all examples of non-chronological reports. The purpose of a non-chronological report is to describe things the way they are. Key text characteristics are:

- opening statement;
- technical language;
- further description;
- written in the present tense;
- uses facts and 'Did you know?' sections to create interest;
- pictures and diagrams add further detail.

The spider's web symbol used for non-chronological reports gives a visual representation of the key word with sub-sections coming off the main subject.

36–37 Finding out about the Great Fire of London

Use the text to investigate the questions 'Where?', 'When?', 'Why?', 'What?' and 'Who?' that are answered in the report. These questions are often at the heart of non-fiction texts, as we are finding out information about something, finding the answers to questions. Remind children of the visual model of a non-chronological report. Challenge each group to tackle one question each, extending the information in the text and finding out as much as they can from a variety of sources on their particular aspect. **T13, T14, S6**

38–39 The wheel

This text supports QCA D&T Unit 2A. Explore with the class the title and introductory paragraph. This paragraph contains a lot of technical vocabulary. Use the paragraph to investigate unfamiliar words and model for the class how you write a new introductory paragraph on wheels in your own words. As the unit builds, discuss with the class which information is really useful or interesting and make notes on what you would like to include in your own version as a plan.

Build the report up as the unit develops, modelling how to write using the key features of non-chronological report writing for each fact to support children in their own composition. The introductory paragraph and series of facts could then be assembled into a zigzag booklet for display in the book corner. **T19, T21**

40–41 Traditional tales

This text could be used in conjunction with the traditional tales in the collection of *Classworks Fiction and Poetry Texts*. Use the text to build a poster for the school library or class reading corner to accompany a traditional tale collection. The format could also be applied to 'What is a fairy tale?' or 'What is an adventure story?'.

42–43 Body bits

Links to QCA Science Unit 2A. Non-chronological reports often appear in children's 'finding out' type comics. Explore this example with the class, identifying key features and discussing the way comics use colour and captions to attract the reader. Ask the class to bring in other examples of non-chronological reports from comics or other sources at home. Make a class comic, with each child contributing a non-chronological report on a topic of interest, researched in the library and composed following this structure. Publish for younger children, parents or the school library. **T20, T21**

Texts 44–47 support QCA Science Unit 2B.

44–45 Butterflies and moths

These pages are written to exemplify the key features of a non-chronological report:

- factual title;
- general introductory statement including technical language (latin classification);
- sub-sections of information on various characteristics of butterflies and moths;
- illustrations to give extra detail;
- a 'Did you know?' interesting fact.

Build the unit of work around a giant display with:

- key word in the middle; children's sub-sections coming out from the central circle to inform the reader about various aspects of the topic, arranged in a 'topic web';
- illustrations to accompany the aspects;
- a dramatic 'Did you know?' question at the bottom.

46–47 Spiders

A further example of a science-based non-chronological report. Use to support a unit leading to an outcome where pupils research interesting facts (books, ICT, Internet) about spiders and present them as a report. **T14, T16, T20**

48–49 How did the dinosaurs become extinct?

This report introduces a discursive element into the text. It is a non-chronological report, but on a topic that would support a spoken outcome in the form of a group debate. Read the text with the class and identify the key features of a non-chronological text. Discuss the fact that because this happened so many years ago there are no records of how it actually happened – no humans were alive to see it. Explore the concept of there being a choice of reasons and ask each group to research and make the case for one of the explanations. Provide the class with a range of dinosaur texts and model for them how to skim-read the contents page and index for key words relating to their particular theory. Children could also research their theory on the Internet using a child-friendly website, such as *www.ajkids.com* or *www.yahooligans.com*, both of which have a wealth of information on dinosaur extinction theories.

The children work as a group to collect evidence and assemble it into bullet-pointed notes of key words and phrases to prompt them in preparing a speech arguing their case. Model for the class (with your teaching assistant if you can) how to put forward a case for a particular option, using evidence to back up your points. Work with each group in turn in guided work to support in appointing a spokesperson and fine-tuning theories. Other members of the group could draw pictures to illustrate their option, or make banners to protest against their option.

As an outcome for the unit, organise a spoken presentation for each group, to an audience. Build into the unit specific rules for both speaking and listening and draw up a 'Good speakers' and 'Good listeners' checklist. **T17, T15, T19**

50 A checklist for good speaking and listening

Use this text as a model to discuss, annotate and refine to make a class checklist for good speakers and listeners. This will support Text 49 but can also be used for any other speaking and listening outcomes in any curriculum area. Ref: *QCA Speaking, listening, learning: working with children in Key Stages 1 and 2*. DfES 0626 – 2003 and 0627 – 2003.